Withernsea

A Popular History of a Popular East Yorkshire Seaside Resort

by

John Whitehead

Dedicated
to the
People of Withernsea

Foreword by **A. J. Fouracre**, F.R.C.G.P.

Highgate Publications (Beverley) Ltd

1988

British Library Cataloguing in Publication Data

Whitehead, John
   Withernsea: a popular history of a popular
   East Yorkshire seaside resort.
   1. Humberside. Withernsea, history
   I. Title
   942.8'38

ISBN 0-948929-13-8

ISBN 0 948929 13 8

Published by Highgate Publications (Beverley) Ltd.
24 Wylies Road, Beverley, North Humberside, HU17 7AP
Telephone (0482) 866826

Printed and Typeset in 10 on 11pt Plantin by
B.A. Press, 2-4 Newbegin, Lairgate, Beverley, HU17 8EG
Telephone (0482) 882232

Foreword

Those of us who were born in Withernsea, who have spent our formative years there and even pursued our occupations there, have come to regard the town with an affection which, though often obscured by familiarity and little mentioned because of our northern reserve, is nevertheless deep rooted. With scarcely an imposing building, very ordinary streets, almost treeless, and a bleak though dry climate, at first acquaintance the town has little to commend it. Yet those who come tend to remain or return in later life, blending with long established families and developing a sense of belonging.

Jack Whitehead is one of our sons who, having served his country well, has returned to Withernsea. He developed his interest by giving various talks on the town and now has had the energy, application and perseverance to document the town's history in what will, I feel confident, become recognised as an authoritative opuscule.

We understand him when he refers to 'our funny, ugly, little town'. His mention of the unusually egalitarian society in Withernsea is a good point. Helped by the lack of landed gentry, since the few local landowners are all working farmers, and by the absence of slums, the town is entirely middle class. Thus there are no doors which are closed to the enterprising.

It has always fascinated me that the name of Withernsea is unique. Other Hulls, Beverleys, Grimsbys and Humbers abound — but no more Withernseas. That is not to say that people overseas are unaware of this town, and it has constantly surprised me to find on my travels how many people have Withernsea connections. One reference I did hear of was in Perth, Western Australia, where an expatriot found a new prestigious building which was called the 'Withernsea Project' — but it was being built by a Singapore-Chinese company.

It is a compliment and a privilege to be asked to write the foreword for this very worthwhile undertaking. Jack Whitehead writes with enthusiasm and gusto, so that all will find it easy to read. It is an accurate account of the history of our town and fills an obvious gap in the list of local histories.

Withernsea. September, 1988   Tony Fouracre

A Withernsea landmark — the towers at the entrance of the former pier.

Preface

Although numerous booklets and newspaper articles on specific aspects of Withernsea's past have been written, it would appear that the town's complete history has not been recorded in one publication. A number of Withernsea people have asked me to rectify this omission and this book is my attempt to meet that need.

As the sub-title and first paragraph indicate, this production does not pretend to be a detailed history. It is, however, the complete history, in that it starts at the town's earliest beginnings and ends in the present, albeit in skeletal form. It is only at the salient points that I have attempted any detail. To have done otherwise would have produced a tome of over three times the size of this book, which was not my intention.

During my research I was amazed at the volume of material forthcoming; the characters alone are of such interest as to merit a book of their own, and the growth of the town and its builders make fascinating reading. All this, and much more, could be classed as flesh for the skeleton and perhaps could well be added by others at a later date.

This history could never have been written without the help and co-operation of others and I am most grateful to all those who helped in innumerable ways to make it all possible. I wish to mention particularly

Miss Mary Mendham, Mrs. Joan Hoyes, Mr. Harry Verity, Mr. Harry Shaw, Mrs. Phyllis Davies, and the countless old Holderness residents who have regaled me over the years with their glimpses into the past. The following immediately spring to mind, but there are many others and I apologise in advance for not recalling them: the late Frank and Harry Drewery, Frank's son — Jim Drewery, Councillor Harold Turner, Geoffrey Hart, Pete Gallagher, Mrs. R. D. Campbell (Kim Kendall), Gordon Greensides, Wilf Lunn, Mrs. Elma Lunn and Mrs. Kitty Grigg.

I am particularly in the debt of the following for entrusting me with their valuable old photographs and slides: Mr. Paul Baker, Mr. John Dennis, Mr. Geoffrey Hart, Mrs. Marie Stephenson, Mr. Jack Whitaker and Mr. Stanley Wakefield.

I am indebted to the staff of the Local Studies Library, Albion Street, Hull, for their considerable help on many occasions.

My thanks also go to John Markham for his final editing and his sound advice on research techniques.

And last but not least, my thanks go to my wife, Phyllis, for her photographic work and for her unfailing support and encouragement.

I hope that the readers of this publication will enjoy it as much as I have enjoyed writing it, particularly the people of Withernsea, to whom the book is dedicated.

John Whitehead
Withernsea, 1988

Acknowledgements

The drawing of Withernsea in 1891 on page 13 by F. S. Smith is in the collection of Hull City Museums and Art Galleries and is reproduced by kind permission of Hull City Council.

The picture of Anthony Bannister on page 14 is in the Illustrations Collection of the Local Studies Library, Central Library, Hull, and is reproduced by kind permission of Humberside Leisure Services.

Withernsea
A Popular History of a Popular
East Yorkshire Seaside Resort

Despite what some may tell us to the contrary, Withernsea does have a history — a long and varied one, so much so that it cannot be told in any detail within the confines of this book and we must be satisfied with the condensed story of its journey through the centuries.

We first hear of it as the Saxon holding of Whithornsea at the time of Edward the Confessor (1047-66), held by Tostig, the Earl of Northumbria. The name Whithornsea simply means 'white thorn by the water' — the suffix 'sea' or 'sey' indicates inland water (a lake or mere), not the more obvious 'sea'.

In 1065 Tostig was 'cast out' and Edward appointed Earl Morcar in his stead; he had but a few months to enjoy his elevation, as, after the 1066 Norman invasion, William quickly dispossessed the Saxon aristocracy. Drogo de Brevere, who fought with William at Hastings, was rewarded by being created the first Lord of Holderness. He made his seat at Skipsea where he built a large castle, and Whithornsea became the Norman manor of Witforness, which literally means 'white thorn on a promontory' (Holderness).

Most people will have heard of Drogo. He was the nefarious Flemish character who later poisoned his wife and fled the country. His flight can well be understood, considering that his wife was also William's niece. One shudders to think what his fate would have been had the Conqueror ever caught up with him.

Witforness was a manor of moderate size consisting of 18 carucates and 6 oxgangs of arable land. A carucate was the land capable of being handled in one year by one team of oxen, later computed to 100 Norman acres and then to 120 modern acres. Similarly, an oxgang can be calculated to equal 15 modern acres. So we see a farming community of some 2,250 arable acres with additional meadow land and large areas of woodland, rich in game.

Unfortunately there is no record of the manor's population although we do know that it had two priests but no church, so the population would not have been large. Poulson tells us that it probably had a rectory and that one of the priests officiated at the dependent hamlet of Hollym. The township would have been one to two miles from the sea.

Witforness prospered. By the time of King John it had a fine church, dedicated to St. Mary, and in 1343 Edward III granted it a charter for two weekly markets and an annual fair. It would have been a substantial inland market town, situated beside a large mere. At about this time it reverted to its Saxon title of Whithornsea, later to become Withernsea.

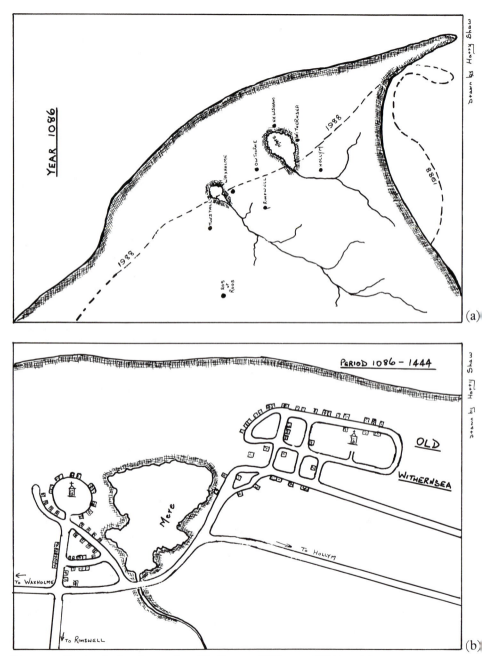

Diagrams to illustrate the changing coastline of Owthorne and Withernsea. [Not to scale]

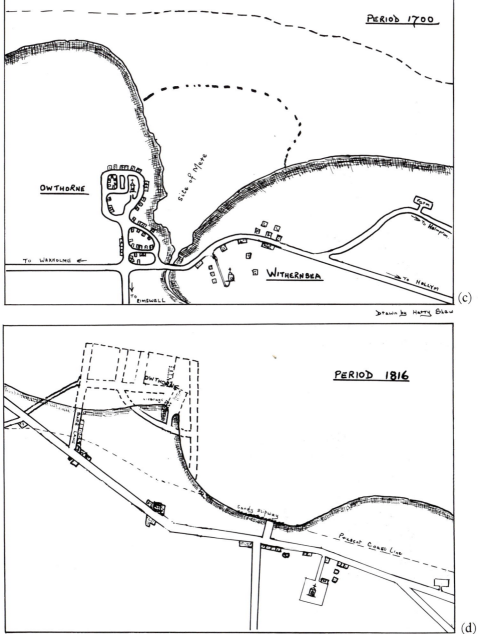

PERIOD 1700

OWTHORNE

Site of Mere

TO WAXHOLME ←

WITHERNSEA

To Holmpton

To Hollym

To RIMSWELL

Drawn by Harry Shaw

(c)

PERIOD 1816

OWTHORNE

Vicarage

Long Lane

Sandy Slipway

Present Coast Line

Drawn by Harry Shaw

(d)

3

The history of the adjoining manor of Owthorne is closely linked with that of Withernsea. Indeed, they eventually became one township. Its modern name is a corruption of 'Outhorne', which simply means 'thorn on the outskirts': it was also known as 'Seathorne'.

Owthorne's church was built at the same time as Withernsea's, of a similar design but slightly smaller. It was dedicated to St. Peter. These two churches have an interesting legend which is worth repeating, with no claim to historical fact. Two sisters each owned a manor and decided that they would build one church to serve both parishes. They quarrelled — one wanted a church with a spire, the other with a tower — and the deadlock was only broken by each sister building her own church. Most legends have some truth behind them and some explanation is required as to why two churches were built within half a mile of each other. Unfortunately, the lie is given to the legend by the fact that neither church ever had a spire. Nevertheless, these churches were always known as the 'sister kirks'.

Ever since the glaciers of the second ice age deposited boulder clay into the ocean to form what is now Holderness, the North Sea has been progressively taking it back, swallowing numerous towns and villages in the process. Thus in the year 1444 the sea eventually caught up with Withernsea, when the church and most of the town were engulfed and disappeared. Evidence points to the fact that this was the time when the sea

St. Nicholas' Church.

4

breached the mere and what was once a mere became a bay. Lord Burghley's Tudor chart, now lodged in the British Museum, shows a pronounced bay at Withernsea, and the Elizabethan edict for the nation's defence against the Spaniards describes this bay and goes on to say, 'from which a creke leads inland where small shyppes may enter and do annoyance'. The mere and the subsequent bay are now thought to have been larger than previously considered, although accurate research is difficult as all evidence is under the sea. This point is worthy of further investigation.

Withernsea cannot have been completely destroyed in 1444, or maybe it was quickly re-built. In either case, by 1488 a new and substantial church, dedicated to St. Nicholas, was completed on a site known as Priest's Hill. This church is still with us today and remains the parish church.

Over the centuries the relentless seas continued to erode Holderness, and Withernsea and Owthorne steadily declined as their farmland disappeared. After the 16th-century Protestant Reformation the churches had financial problems, and by the 17th century the declining parish of Withernsea was becoming hard pressed to maintain its church. In the great storm of 1609 St. Nicholas' Church lost its roof, and, as the parish was too poor to have it repaired, the church remained a picturesque ruin for some 250 years. By the turn of the 19th century both towns were reduced to hamlets, their combined population being only 272.

Withernsea was still in a bay, but one greatly reduced; more accurately, it could be described as a cliffless sandy cove. The northern headland, on which huddled the remains of the once prosperous township of Owthorne, still protected it from the worst of the northern gales. Owthorne church remained standing and in use, but not for long. In 1801 it was replaced by a new church, dedicated to St. Mary, about a mile inland at Rimswell. By 1816 St. Peter's Church at Owthorne was no more — it had survived for almost 400 years longer than its sister kirk at Withernsea but its high cliffs and rising ground could not hold out against the North Sea forever. The corpses and coffins littering the beach and protruding from the cliff face were dutifully re-interred at Rimswell.

St. Peter's Church, Owthorne.

In the early 19th century Withernsea was described as 'a long straggling village on the sea cliff containing 850 acres of land'. So it is not surprising that its history is closely connected to, and influenced by, the sea. Nevertheless, it was always essentially an agricultural community, the fishing families being a latter-day minority.

There is little doubt that Withernsea and Owthorne were livelier places in the late 18th and early 19th centuries than one might at first assume. They were, surprisingly, communities of very young people with large families; for example, Thomas Coleman had seven children, Mary Simpson eight, John Smith five, Thomas Wright five and Frances Grindell six. According to the 1841 census, over 70% of the population were aged twenty and under, and it appears certain that the children formed an essential labour force for the family farms. What comes through from reports and anecdotes is a young, rumbustious and vigorous village community whose people cheerfully accepted their hard but free life. They had known no other and in no way felt deprived; no one had remembered to tell them how poor they were! These two coastal villages also had their moments of drama. One example is given in Appendix A.

As early as Tudor times there are records of the North Sea being England's main artery of commerce between the North and the South. All manner of goods, from grain and timber to linen and clothing, moved along this medieval highway, and in particular the ever-increasing coal trade from the northern mines to London and beyond. Many of the ships carrying this cargo were unseaworthy, mere rotting hulks, nicknamed coffin ships, and the Holderness coastline was the graveyard of many of these decrepit vessels. The wrecks were so numerous that only the more spectacular merited a mention in the newspapers of the 19th century; 200 ships lost on the Yorkshire coast in one storm was not an unusual report.

Over the centuries, the people of Withernsea and Owthorne plundered many of these wrecks without conscience. The Good Lord may not have sent them manna from Heaven but other treasures from the sea He supplied in abundance, and if the odd corpse was found amongst the débris, well, that was God's will, and had to be accepted along with other pestilences. If we are tempted to judge our forebears too hastily in this, we must remember that that was the whole nation's attitude in those early days and that a few good wrecks made all the difference between full stomachs and a cold and hungry winter. Yet almost overnight, it would seem, these coastal people had a dramatic change of heart — they became dedicated sea rescuers — Why? Perhaps it was because they had turned to the sea for food and had become fishermen, thereby having an affinity with the shipwrecked mariners.

It is impossible to give an exact date, but certainly by the 1840s over a dozen families were actively fishing off Withernsea, some with two or three boats per family. Many of the early fishermen were immigrants from

An early picture of a rocket life-saving brigade team, with rocket and handcart c.1890. Note (left) the line slingers' throwing stick and line.

Norfolk who brought their own boats with them. How did they come? Did they sail up the coast and land on the beaches like Vikings? If not, they should have done — but we shall never know. Come they certainly did, and their family names are still remembered — the Bishops, Houpalls, Parkinsons, Quintons and others. The friendly rivalry regarding the merits and de-merits of the local cobles and the Norfolk Sheringhams are still recalled by the descendants of the fishing fraternity.

Whatever the reason, these hardy fisherfolk were now dedicated to saving lives and took great pride in their skill and daring. In addition, none of the rescued ever lacked succour. A room was set aside in the one hostelry of Withernsea and Owthorne specifically for the comfort of rescued seamen, where a hot meal and warm blankets were permanently available. (This would have been the *Neptune,* situated on the present site of the *Spread Eagle*). In the case of multiple wrecks, some victims were cared for in the fishermen's own homes. All this without Government aid or outside sponsorship! They used their own boats and equipment and, of course, received no pay.

These self-appointed saviours had three distinct methods of rescue. The first was by boats, before the stricken vessel struck the beach. When conditions made this impossible, another method would be to get a line aboard the grounded ship before it broke up — no mean feat, considering that their open boats had to be rowed out through the raging surf. A strong rope was fed from the line, along which the victims would be hauled to safety. They would probably have been seated in a rope or canvas harness, similar to that later known as the breeches-buoy (invented by George Manby in 1856). To facilitate this operation a three-legged gin was rigged ashore, preferably on the cliff top, with a two-way pulley system, on which all hands would heave. In many instances a pair of plough horses was used, particularly during severe storms. Thirdly, when all else failed, these safety lines were thrown by hand. They were weighted by an egg-shaped lump of lead connected to a two-foot throwing stick, and could be flung prodigious distances with unerring accuracy. The object was to strike the mast, when the weight would wrap the line tightly round it.

These 'line slingers', as they were known, became increasingly proficient and 'line slinging' developed into a local sport, being a prominent event at all shows and meetings. The one who secured the line, (and it had to be tightly secured) round a representative mast (known as the 'wreck post') from the greatest distance was the winner. They practised incessantly and even gambled on their weekly competitions. A champion line slinger was hero-worshipped by the local youths in much the same way as a star footballer is today and the sport continued long after it was needed for sea rescue, almost until living memory.

☆　☆　☆　☆　☆

Launching the lifeboat, using heavy horses.

The new church at Rimswell soon proved itself to be too distant for convenience and the parishioners of Owthorne complained of the long trudge to worship, particularly during the winter months. In 1850 a chapel of ease was built in Waxholme Road (now Queen Street) directly opposite Barb Lane (now North Gate), which solved the problem. As one vicar served both places of worship, a rectory was built in Hull Road, midway between the two. It is still with us today, the private residence of Mr. and Mrs. Brian Nordon. This 'temporary' arrangement continued for over eighty years until the new Owthorne church, St. Matthew's, was built in Hull Road in 1934/35. The architects were Milner and Craze of London. This explains to puzzled visitors why Withernsea has two churches.

Although Withernsea and Owthorne have long since been a single township, ecclesiastically Owthorne remains a separate parish from Withernsea, although one vicar serves both churches. St. Mary's Church, built in 1801 at Rimswell, is now accepted as Rimswell's church, its origin as Owthorne's second church being confined to the mists of history. Incidentally, it is one of the few Georgian churches in East Yorkshire.

Wesleyan Methodism came early to Owthorne. In 1809 a tiny chapel was established in Barb Lane: probably the cobbled cottage now situated at No. 4, Northgate. The Circuit, centred on Patrington, had 335 members on inception, but dissension was on the way and soon the organisation became split.

In 1810 Hugh Bourn, from the Stafford Potteries Methodist Group, led a breakaway faction after the style of American evangelists, and from this, in 1812, was born the Primitive Methodist Society, when their first chapel was built at Tunstall (Staffordshire). By 1841 the cult had spread to Withernsea, and the Withernsea Primitive Methodist Society was formed in 1848 with three members — Grice Jackson, George Hunter and R. W. Dry. They met for prayer meetings and occasional services in their respective houses until they could afford a chapel. Funds were eventually raised and in 1858 a chapel was built in Alma Street.

In the same year the Wesleyans built their second chapel in what is now Cammidge Street, within hailing distance of Alma Street. This was the recurring pattern throughout the country; the two societies were in constant competition and built chapels adjacent to each other when one would have sufficed for both congregations. In 1879 the Primitive Methodists opened their second and last chapel in Hull Road. It remains today and is in active use. The Alma Street premises are now used as a bus garage.

By the turn of the 20th century the Wesleyan congregation had long since outgrown its Cammidge Street chapel and in 1900/1 a magnificent church was opened by the Wesleyans in Queen Street; the earlier chapel was demolished. With its finely proportioned architecture and high steeple it was one of the few impressive buildings in Withernsea. Notwithstanding the competition between the two factions, the builder of this fine Wesleyan

Wesleyan Church, Queen Street, 1901.

church was W.N. Carr, the chapel steward of the Primitive Methodists! In those hard-headed days, religion was not allowed to interfere with business.

By the 1920s the two separate branches of Methodism had slowly learnt to work in harmony and in 1932 they agreed to a scheme of union. In Withernsea this was wisely taken one step at a time, and it was not until the 1960s that complete amalgamation was achieved and the one chapel agreed.

Despite its impressive appearance, the Wesleyan church in Queen Street was not as structurally sound as the Hull Road chapel and it was decided that the latter should be adopted as the joint place of worship. And so, despite a few dissenters, principally at Holmpton, Methodism became a united religion and still continues as such, with a flourishing following.

The grand edifice in Queen Street was demolished in 1961 and Withernsea lost one of its few buildings of dignity and beauty. Sheltered accommodation for the elderly has recently been built on the site, and, sensitively, named Wesley Court; and so the name of that great religious reformer lives on in Withernsea.

In 1903 the Congregational church was established at Withernsea, at first in a schoolroom, until a church was built later at the corner of Lee Avenue. In 1972 it united with the Presbyterian Church of England to become the United Reformed Church. It is still active as such today.

After the emancipation of the Catholic faith in 1829, Catholic churches were established throughout the kingdom. The handful of Catholics at Withernsea had to travel to Hull or Hedon for Sunday mass, so in 1906 Bishop Lacy arranged for one of the Hull priests to say mass in a small café at the resort. Soon after, a tiny wooden church was built, and when the Marist Fathers came to Hull they took responsibility for the Catholics of Withernsea. In May, 1936, Withernsea was established as a parish when a newly built church in Bannister Street was blessed by Dr. McAuley, S.M., the first parish priest being Father (later Canon) Wood. This church, dedicated to St. Peter and St. John Fisher, is the most southerly one of the

Diocese of Middlesbrough. It was designed personally by Bishop Shine and was built by F. Spink of Bridlington. It cost £1,045!

Regular services still continue in this small but beautiful church.

☆　　☆　　☆　　☆　　☆

Early in the 19th century, the nation was swept by two social events which vitally influenced the future of Withernsea. They have been aptly described as twin manias — railway mania and seaside mania.

In the 17th and 18th centuries health spas were popular with the aristocracy and fashionable society who would descend upon such places as Bath and Harrogate to take the health-giving waters. These towns became places of high fashion with theatres, assembly rooms and gardens. It was claimed that the waters cured all ills, including leprosy!

In 1626 Scarborough became a spa and quickly grew in size and opulence. Unlike other spas, its small spring did not lend itself to bathing and so, with typical enterprise, sea water (or the briny) was claimed as being equally beneficial and the wealthy clients were dunked daily, with due ceremony, by their hirelings. The small village of Brighton became established as a sea-bathing spa and quickly prospered. When it was patronised by royalty (the Prince Regent, later George IV), 'watering places', not yet 'seaside resorts', became fashionable and rapidly replaced the health spas in popularity; but they were still the preserve of the social élite.

After the 1830s it seemed that everyone was building railways from

Withernsea in 1863. [From a painting by George Cammidge.]
Note Queen's Hotel in background and the bay clearly visible.

Withernsea from the south, 1891, by F. S. Smith. [Hull City Council].

everywhere to anywhere. Companies were floated and lines sprang up almost overnight, which made a tremendous impact on the social life of the nation. With the arrival of the railways, seaside resorts came within the reach of a wider population and seaside mania had begun; although, at first, the resorts were mainly patronised by the expanding middle classes.

And now the future of Withernsea was in the hands of one man, Anthony Bannister. A typical thrusting early Victorian entrepreneur, he was a prominent merchant and ship owner with many commercial interests in the rapidly expanding town of Hull. His portrait shows him as a heavily bearded, stern-faced patriarch and yet, when Anthony Bannister brought the railway to Withernsea,

Anthony Bannister.
[Humberside Leisure Services]

he was a mere thirty-seven years old and had already been the mayor of Hull (1852); this was indeed the age of the young.

He now realised that railways could be a source of further fame and fortune and floated a company to capture the beef and corn trade in Holderness. Holderness was a high yielding agricultural area and its produce had always been transported inland by river from the haven at Patrington. With the rapid emergence of Sunk Island, Patrington Haven was quickly becoming silted up and Bannister realised that a railway from Hull, through the various villages to Patrington, was a profitable proposition.

He decided to couple this venture with a terminus on the coast where Hull's own seaside town could be established, with, of course, tremendous profits for himself and his colleagues. The sandy, cliffless cove at Withernsea, still partially protected from the North and with easy access to the beach, was finally selected, although Easington and Tunstall had also been considered. The railway was built ahead of schedule and was formally opened on 26 June, 1854.

The company's first train was standing on its new line at Paragon Station, gaily decorated and in scroll work bearing the words, 'Success to Hull and Holderness Railway'. Over five hundred invitations had been issued for this initial journey and the long train eventually pulled out of the station at 11.20

The former Queen's Hotel and Railway Station.

am (twenty minutes late!) Crowds had gathered at all the colourfully decorated stations along the route and at Hedon the church bells rang out as if in welcome — the whole of Holderness was in the grip of railway fever.

On arrival at Withernsea, officials and guests assembled in a large marquee for the celebration luncheon. Anthony Bannister, as the chairman, was seated between the Rt. Hon. Lord Londesborough and the Hon. Arthur Duncombe M.P. It was a wet and windy day and during the meal a third of the marquee blew down — an omen? Nothing daunted, the distinguished company re-arranged themselves and settled down to enjoy the speeches and toasts. Thirteen toasts were proposed and replied to and the general atmosphere was one of optimism and confidence in the new venture. No one doubted that the Hull and Holderness Railway would flourish and be a profitable concern. The celebrations ended at 4.00 pm and, after a stroll along the sea front (the rain had apparently ceased), the assembly entrained for the return journey, arriving safely at 7.00 pm.

The railway had come to Withernsea and things would never be the same again.

☆　　☆　　☆　　☆　　☆

We now briefly leave Withernsea and go to the Isle of Man, where a certain Sir William Hillary had retired after many years in the Mediterranean. He was horrified by the wrecks and loss of life near his home, and, being a small boat expert, saved many lives with scratch crews in his own boat. In the year 1822, after losing two boats and almost his life, he devised and had built a boat specifically for saving lives; he called it a lifeboat. The idea caught on and others made donations for life-boats around the coasts, and in 1824 the National Life-Boat Institution was born — dependent entirely on charitable donations, as it is to this day. (The National Life-Boat Institution is now the Royal National Lifeboat Institution).

And so, in 1862, the self-appointed lifeboat men of Withernsea received their reward — the first of Withernsea's five renowned lifeboats. It was donated by Miss Sarah Lechmere, a clergyman's daughter from Worcestershire, and was named *Pelican* after the Lechmere family crest. Messrs. Forrest of Limehouse were the builders, at a cost of £300. The boat house was erected in what is now Arthur Street by Alfred Brown of Hull, using local labour, and was described in a newspaper report as being 'commodious and substantial'. It is still there, now used as offices by the D.H.S.S.

The new lifeboat was ceremoniously launched on Monday, 15 August, 1862, before a huge crowd of well wishers. According to one newspaper an estimated 20,000 people attended! They came by train, by horse and carriage, on foot and by sea. Several yachts and sailing boats carrying small parties arrived from Hull, and the gaily decorated fire steamer, *Zebra*, carrying 400 passengers, left Hull from Corporation Pier at ten o'clock — the weather was reported as being 'splendidly unclouded'.

After the Rev. G. C. Pearse of Paull had offered up a prayer the procession started from the boathouse for the beach at 4.00 pm. It was led by the wives of the crew, wearing white caps and carrying small white banners. The fifteen crew members, wearing new cork life belts, were seated in their allotted positions in the boat which was drawn on its specially designed carriage by eight horses. Of course, a band was in attendance. On arrival at the beach the boat was formally christened by Miss Champney (the daughter of Withernsea's first R.N.L.I. chairman) who broke a bottle of wine over its bow. After a smooth launching, the crew pulled speedily out to the *Zebra* where the lifeboat was capsized and her self-righting properties were demonstrated. Later the crew were treated to a sumptuous supper at the expense of Miss Lechmere — and so ended a momentous day in the history of Withernsea.

For the next fifteen years *Pelican* and her crews did sterling work, saving a total of 42 lives, before being replaced by a new boat, *Admiral Rouse*, in 1877. Unfortunately Miss Lechmere died before her lifeboat had saved any lives.

In 1883 Withernsea acquired its third lifeboat, *Admiral Rouse II*, when a new boathouse was built in Seaside Road. It is now an amusement arcade, opposite the Pier Hotel. The R.N.L.I. presented the old Arthur Street

The Lifeboat Crew, late 19th century. Note the leather sea-boots and cork jackets.

An early emergency.

18

boathouse to the Coast Guards as their Rocket, or Life Saving Brigade, Headquarters, where their rocket apparatus could be stored. For some years these Rocket Brigades had been set up around Britain's coastline by the Board of Trade, their members being recruited locally. So the intrepid line slingers had for some time been equipped with rockets, lines, tools and a hand cart; but, more importantly, they had been officially recognised as professionals under the guidance of the Coast Guards. Their exploits with hand lines had passed into history.

☆　　☆　　☆　　☆　　☆

The railway, as we have seen, had arrived at Withernsea in 1854. We should now look at the next stage of our story. The ambitions for this new seaside resort were boundless. It was to be a second Filey or even Scarborough. The railway handbook shows clearly that the intention was to attract a distinguished and refined clientèle and to this end Cuthbert Brodrick was engaged as the railway architect. He was later to become famous as the designer of Leeds Town Hall and the Grand Hotel, Scarborough. The designs for Withernsea were elegant and ambitious — a grand Station Hotel, boulevards, promenades, crescents, tree-lined avenues and assembly rooms — in fact, a second Filey. It was never built — the sum total of development was the station, the Station Hotel (named the Queen's) and a gas works wherewith to light them. Although the hotel was described as the 'Station Hotel' on the initial plans, it was named the 'Queen's' on its opening, most probably to commemorate the visit of Queen Victoria to Hull in 1854, an occasion on which Bannister had presented the loyal address.

The hotel cost £10,530. It was a luxurious building of forty bedrooms, standing in its own grounds with well laid out gardens and a clear and uninterrupted view of the German Ocean (renamed the North Sea in 1914). This building is well up to Brodrick's later designs and Withernsea is fortunate in that it still stands.

At first all went well. In the first four months over 63,000 passengers used the line and all seemed set for success. This new seaside resort, however, could not be without a substantial place of worship for its elegant guests, and the ruined church of St. Nicholas was hardly in keeping with the town's anticipated new status; so after much deliberation it was decided to re-build the church to its former glory. Public subscriptions were called for and the Holderness Railway Company led the list with a large donation.

The church was re-built in its old tradition, chiefly of beach cobble stones, with quarried stone for the chancel, buttresses and battlements, and the old bells, being lost, were replaced by a single bell in the western tower. The restored church of St. Nicholas was re-dedicated on 1 June, 1859, the total cost of restoration being in the region of £12,000. There are now seven bells in the church — the last being donated in 1948. Bathing machines were also set up on the beach by the railway company, which also offered special facilities for anyone building at Withernsea. But build for themselves they did not; they preferred to sell the land already purchased, at a profit, to others who were willing to risk their money. In other words, they lost their nerve and the grandiose schemes were abandoned.

One must have some sympathy with them. After the first rush, probably from curiosity, the rich and distinguished failed to arrive and it was soon evident that the new hotel was to become a white elephant; it was already running at a loss.

We should understand that the sole interest of Bannister and his co-directors was financial and there was no money to be made from empty hotels. Their problem was one of timing. To attract a rich clientèle they required more than one luxurious hotel and a sandy cove, but without this patronage they could not finance their grand schemes — indeed, a cleft stick situation. Scarborough, of course, already had its magnificent facilities from the days of the spa.

It was fortuitous that plans for the restoration of the church were made during the first flush of enthusiasm. Nevertheless, Withernsea owes a great debt to these ambitious entrepreneurs for their initiative. Without them St.

Queen Street from the south, c.1890, showing the Commercial Hotel, formerly the Sailor's Return.

Nicholas' Church would most probably have remained a derelict ruin for many more years.

And there things rested — a railway to nowhere with the future in considerable doubt. Fortunately history is seldom made by the planners, but by people, and the people of Hull took over Withernsea and made it their own.

☆　☆　☆　☆　☆

It is almost impossible to envisage the squalor of our towns and cities in the mid-19th century. The filth, smoke and stench in the overcrowded alleys and courts of Hull were indescribable. People were born there and they died there without ever seeing the green countryside, let alone the sea. They knew no other life and largely accepted their lot — and now, presented to them some one hour's journey away, was paradise — fresh air, sea, clean sandy beaches and space to run free. It was Treasure Island and Coral Island rolled into one, and they came literally in their thousands. They needed no assembly halls and rich facades for their entertainment; nature provided for all their needs.

Initially only the merchants, tradesmen and skilled artisans could afford the fare and it was they who were the early citizens of the new town. They came first for the day, then with their families for the weekend, and then gradually extended their visits until they either rented or had built their summer seaside homes. Why not? Travel was cheap and the journey short. It was only a small step forward for them to transfer their homes to Withernsea and the commuter age had begun.

In the summer season finding holiday accommodation was not difficult; it would seem that almost everyone 'took in visitors'; they were not boarding house keepers, but ordinary housewives who catered for whole families at reasonable rates. Many visitors came year after year and became lifelong friends of their hosts. Others caught the fever and settled in the town to become commuters. A few boarding houses sprang up and, much later, a large hotel (another Queen's) was built in 1901, but most visitors preferred to stay with private families.

The railway company offered exceptionally cheap day return tickets and the poorer people could now afford an occasional visit to the seaside; it was then that the thousands of day 'trippers', previously mentioned, began to pour into Withernsea. Special excursions were run by the railway company at weekends and holidays to cater for this ever-increasing demand. But, despite this heavy patronage, the Hull and Holderness Railway Company was not a financial success. It was too small a concern to be viable and in 1860, only six years after its inception, it was first taken over on lease by the giant North Eastern Railway, and then absorbed two years later. This company permitted free travel to its employees and their families, which resulted in a large railway community being added to Withernsea's already expanding population.

The 1861 census showed that the population had more than doubled to 626 and it was still increasing. This increase in population brought prosperity and the two villages were quickly expanding into a single township. At first most of the building was in the Owthorne area, although the linear development had joined the two villages together. It was all unplanned and haphazard. Some houses fronted the streets, others stood well back; they were built to individual tastes and requirements and were all of different shapes and sizes — in fact the town was becoming an architectural muddle. The roads were unmetalled, street lighting was non-existent, the drainage was becoming inadequate and the water supply was from a few wells and pumps.

The town needed taking in hand if it were not to degenerate into chaos. Before discussing how this was done, we will consider the type of society that was forming at Withernsea in the late 1860s. Its population was becoming clearly defined into three groups:

1. The original residents — farmers, agricultural workers and fishermen, supplemented by workers, largely immigrants, employed in the town's development.

2. The commuters, mainly tradespeople, business men, a few teachers, railwaymen and clerical workers — all employed in Hull.

Edwardian Withernsea.

22

3. The entrepreneurs (not Bannister and his colleagues) who came to build and stayed on; also shopkeepers and publicans.

In addition there was an influx of wealthy merchants who later were to have great influence on the tone and organisation of the town — at one time the sheriff of Hull, Robert Metcalf, lived at Withernsea.

The residents of this mushrooming town were now established. They identified themselves with it and were concerned for its future. That it needed to be improved was not in doubt and in 1871 the Withernsea Improvement Company, or, to give it its full title, the Withernsea Pier, Gas and General Improvement Company Ltd., was formed. Its prospectus was published in 1872 and we note with interest that Anthony Bannister was the chairman. He had brought the railway to Withernsea some eighteen years before and had then abandoned his ambitious plans for the construction of a seaside resort. Moreover, the railway company had been out of his control for over ten years. So what was the reason for his renewed interest? Was it all his idea or was he co-opted by the originators because of his name?

Certainly, the company's plans for the resort's development were pure Bannister. They were almost as flamboyant as the earlier ones, and if they had been carried out Withernsea would have rivalled any other resort in its magnificence. It was even planned to build a fish dock at Withernsea, whereby fish could be transported directly to Hull by rail, obviating the long and often dangerous haul up the Humber by the fishing fleets. Anyone who has seen green water breaking over Withernsea's sea walls during winter storms will appreciate the sheer lunacy of such a scheme.

Whether Bannister was the leading force or not, other members of the board had interests in Withernsea apart from financial gain, and wiser counsel appears to have taken control. The elaborate schemes were shelved for more practical plans and by 1876 much had been achieved and the town was considerably improved. Five groynes were built to protect the beach from further erosion, a gas works was planned, the roads were repaired and metalled and the new houses being erected, whilst not exactly elegant, were of a good pattern and built to an approved specification. Drainage was now adequate and in its brochures the town could even boast of its pure water supply.

In 1873 Withernsea had its first newspaper, the *Withernsea Chronicle*, printed in Hull. An early edition — No. 71 — dated Saturday, 8 August, 1874, includes many revealing reports of life at Withernsea in the early days of its development. The text of one on water supply is of particular interest and is quoted below:

WITHERNSEA — THE WATER SUPPLY — A great want of good water (indeed in many cases of any water at all) has long been felt by some of the inhabitants of this village; we are glad therefore to see a new pump erected over the old well, from which, we are informed, there was always an abundant supply. This work has been done at a cost of about £5, and on the responsibility of Mr. Batty and Mr. D. Stephenson. Numbers no doubt will derive a benefit from their forethought, and will not allow those gentlemen to be out of pocket, by trying to assist the inhabitants to so great a boon as a good supply of water must be.

This pump is almost certainly the one remembered by older inhabitants at the junction of Seaside Road and Queen Street. There are still Battys and Stephensons in the district — possibly descendants of these two benefactors.

In 1891 the *Withernsea Chronicle* closed down and Withernsea was without a newspaper until 1910. It was then that a journalist, formerly of the *Driffield Times*, Arthur Edward Lunn, published his first edition of the *Withernsea Times* as Withernsea's only newspaper. It was a weekly edition, delivered free to all households; in 1923 its name was changed to the *Withernsea Gazette*. For many years Arthur Lunn ran a family business; he was the publisher, editor and distributor. He also set up his own printing presses in premises in Walter Street, which were later removed to Seaside Road. This printing business remained in the same building and still under the name of Lunn until 1987. Arthur Lunn died in 1934, when his youngest son, John Wilfred Lunn, took over at the tender age of 21. The printing works and the newspaper continued to prosper and eventually reached a distribution figure of over 2,000 copies. It had become the eyes and ears of Withernsea. At the outbreak of war in 1939 most of the men, including the proprietor, went to war, and the newspaper was discontinued in 1940. But not the printing works; this went on as before under the stewardship of Mr. Lunn's wife, Elma.

In 1946, despite problems of supply, Wilf Lunn re-published his paper. He even extended it to cover the whole of Holderness, re-titled it the *Holderness Gazette* and charged 1d per copy; the distribution figure then rose to 6,500 copies. In 1980 Mr. John Wilfred Lunn retired and the *Holderness Gazette* passed into other hands. It was bought by a consortium of three professional newspaper men who continue to produce this informative and, in many ways, unique little newspaper in the true tradition of its founder, Mr. Arthur Lunn. It now costs 20p per copy!

☆   ☆   ☆   ☆   ☆

After 1876 the Withernsea Improvement Company could now turn its attention to less mundane matters. For some years seaside resorts around the coast had discovered that people took pleasure in strolling along piers and jetties and it was decided to build pleasure piers purely for the entertainment of visitors. Saloons and seating were provided, and usually a

The Edwardian crowded beach.

small charge was made. All around England pleasure piers sprouted like unrimmed spokes of a wheel, and no self-respecting Victorian seaside resort could be without one. Withernsea *had* to have a pier and the Improvement Company made its plans accordingly. It was also decided to build a protective sea wall and an ornamental promenade.

Before discussing these events further we will consider the characters of the men responsible. The directors of the company named in their 1872 prospectus include a large proportion of local men. The vice-chairman was a certain James Young Esq., a resident of Owthorne. We can find little information about him, except that he was a man of substance. He was probably a Hull merchant or a professional man. It is noted that in the directors' report of 1879 he was recorded as 'the retiring Chairman, on rotation, together with his son, eligible for re-election'. Thomas Alban MacManus Esq., M.R.C.S., L.S.A., of Withernsea, was another: obviously a man of education and standing. Although the next director's address was given as Hull, he appears, later in 1893, as the chairman of the Withernsea Branch of the R.N.L.I. — Horatio Harriman Ayr, a much respected local man. All were Withernsea men and therefore all were personally involved in the town's future.

There is no further mention of Anthony Bannister after the first few years and it would appear that he had left the arena. These new men were more modest and less ebullient than the earlier entrepreneurs; they had adopted

Withernsea as their home and with the support of the townspeople were unobtrusively setting about to develop it on sound principles.

However, we must not forget Anthony Bannister and the great debt owed to him by Withernsea. Although in some ways he failed in his ambitions, it was he who brought the railway to Withernsea and without him the town would never have existed as it is today. Indeed, it is most probable that Withernsea and Owthorne would now be featured amongst the 'lost towns of Holderness'. It is fitting that Bannister Street in Withernsea bears his name, and sad that he never lived to see it. He died in 1878 at his home in Hessle at the comparatively young age of 61, the year that the pier and the promenade were opened.

In 1877, the pier and the promenade were completed and in the summer of the following year they were opened to the public. Entry to the pier cost one penny; the promenade was free.

1878 was a gala year. The pier and promenade established Withernsea as a seaside resort, the foundation stones for the new Methodist chapel were laid and the Owthorne Board School was opened in Hull Road. Note the 'Owthorne' — although the two villages had been merging for some years, they were still officially two separate parishes and the school was, in fact, within the Owthorne boundary.

The establishment of the school was a direct result of W. E. Forster's Elementary Education Act of 1870, whereby Board Schools were established throughout the land. These schools were locally run but partly state financed; with Withernsea's expansion the need for more school places was vital. On 12 August, 1875, Withernsea's newly elected School Board met for the first time to select a suitable site for its Board School, although it was officially entitled Owthorne School Board. A full year later, in August, 1876, a site on Hull Road was agreed upon and tenders were invited. That of a local builder, Robert Carr, was accepted in February, 1877, and building began without further delay at an estimated cost of £1,398 — the final cost was £2,000. The architect was J. T. Webster of Hedon.

The school was duly opened in March, 1878, and consisted of one large classroom, a boardroom and the headmaster's room. The capacity of the school was for 150 pupils, although only 103 were enrolled on the first day. It must be remembered, however, that compulsory attendance was not instituted until 1880, and school pence were still levied from parents until 1891. The school staff consisted of the headmaster, Mr. Joseph Sissons, and Miss Theresa Taffinder as the sewing mistress. By March, 1879, the school roll had increased and Mr. Sissons was given an assistant, a Mr. Ferret. Staff problems arose almost immediately. Miss Taffinder resigned in 1878 and was replaced by Mrs. Hardy, who also resigned in July, 1879, with much acrimony. Mr. Ferret was eventually sacked for drunkenness!

In spite of his initial problems, Mr. Sissons progressed and served the school well until retiring in 1913 after 35 years' service. From school

Owthorne Board School in the 1880's. The headmaster, Mr. Sissons (right).

photographs of the 1880s/1890s the children appear to be robust and remarkably well turned out (perhaps Sunday Best for the camera?). In this period we see many changes. By the turn of the century, the school had five members of staff and in December, 1902, an Act of Parliament abolished School Boards and brought Board Schools under the control of the local education authority. Owthorne Board School was now re-named Withernsea Council School.

Almost from the start the numbers of pupils were constantly outgrowing their school. In 1891 there were 140 pupils; by 1893 the number had risen to 210, and, as the school was designed only for 150, urgent action was required. So, in the same year, an extension with extra classrooms was quickly erected by John Wilkinson at a cost of £595. This eased the situation, but classes, by modern standards, were incredibly large: one inspection in 1909 shows a class of 85! The school's growing numbers soon merited a separate infants' department. This was installed in 1903 under Miss Annie Louisa Heath, who was replaced by Miss A. Nibbs in 1905.

Further extensions were made in 1907, and between 1913 and 1915 when the number of pupils had risen to 287. By 1921 the school was so crowded that the two top classes had to be taught in the hall — a class at either end. The situation was eased when the new Withernsea Central School was opened on 5 September, 1921. It consisted of two ex-Army wooden huts in an E shape with an open verandah on the eastern side. Mr. Durrant, who had replaced Mr. Sissons in 1913, moved there with the two top classes and their teachers.

The huts were replaced in 1934 by a new building for the seniors, which served them well for the next twenty years before becoming the junior school in 1954. The seniors then moved to their new school to the west of the old building; this new school was designated 'Withernsea High School'.

And that is how it stands today. We have moved from one school of 103 pupils in 1878 to three schools with a combined student strength of 1705 in 1988.

Who dares to say that Withernsea has not progressed?

☆   ☆   ☆   ☆   ☆

We now return to the promenade and the pier. The promenade was 400 yards in length and stretched from the ancient slipway (immediately opposite Seaside Road) northwards. At its northern end it abutted onto the north cliff.

The sea wall, on which the promenade rested, was made of concrete, re-inforced with old ships' anchor cables. Despite pessimistic forecasts from outside the town that it would crumble into the sea within two years, it has remained defiant for almost 110 years and it still stands today, a monument to its Victorian builders.

The promenade, with its graceful outer wall, is constructionally much the same today as it was in 1878, but aesthetically it is much changed. What is now a road was 400 yards of lawn with a paved promenade to the seaward side and pleasantly sloping flower beds on the other. In the centre between the flower beds was an elegant band stand with an ogee roof; the bandsmen would have faced the sea and the promenade. The Gap, resembling an old pinfold, which is there today, indicates exactly the position of the bandstand, although the bandstand was not completed in its final form until 1901.

Victorian and Edwardian photographs show the crowds promenading in their elegant attire. They had come to see and be seen: a veritable fashion parade.Of course, vehicles were forbidden entry. Withernsea now has almost two miles of promenade but this Victorian centre of 400 yards is by far the most elegant and impressive. The Withernsea Improvement Company's prospectus of 1872 included a pier which, along with the rest of the scheme, never materialized. It would have been in the centre of the promenade, immediately opposite what is now Young Street. The entrance to the pier of 1878 was further south, directly opposite the station: a welcoming sight on first stepping off the train.

This pier was an ambitious venture, built at a cost of £12,000. The contractor was a Mr. O. Gardener and the engineer was Thomas Cargill. The latter specialized in piers and was of high repute; he had previously built the pier at Aldeburgh in Suffolk.

Withernsea's pier was 1,196 feet long, which is just short of a quarter of

A rare photograph of the Pier.

a mile. It was built entirely of iron, except for the entrance which was brick. The uprights used were Mitchell's newly invented screw piles which could be driven deep and quickly into the clay bed below the sand. Along the pier were seats and side shows and at the extreme end were a large saloon and hall for the usual seaside entertainments.

The entrance consisted of two castellated towers, claimed to be a miniature replica of Conway Castle in Wales. Cargill excavated a tunnel under the towers leading to an exit below the pier floor and so on to the beach. This had two advantages:

(1) It ensured that the foundations of the pier towers were deeply supported in the clay.

(2) Maintenance could be carried out without excavation.

That the towers are still standing after over a century of North Sea battering is proof of his expertise; built of brick on sand, a lesson to all embryo civil engineers.

In 1879 the Pier Hotel, newly built in Seaside Road, formerly Outgate, opened its doors to the public and further added to Withernsea's status as a resort.

☆   ☆   ☆   ☆   ☆

So fortune seemed set fair for the future of Withernsea and its latest acquisitions; but the North Sea had other plans! Its influence on the town's history now re-asserted itself and we shall see how its destruction of one man's works brought about the birth of another.

By the 1860s the shipwrecks and loss of life along the Yorkshire coast had reached epic proportions. The rotten, ill-founded condition of many of these vessels, together with their gross overloading, had become a national scandal and yet officialdom seemed powerless to act.

Fortunately, at about this time, the great Victorian conscience was awakening and many social reforms were being mooted. One such reformer was Samuel Plimsoll, a Radical M.P. for Bristol. He had long been pressing for a law to protect seamen and improve their conditions of work. The wealthy and powerful ship and mine owners had successfully blocked his efforts until an event in 1871 completely changed the situation.

On 9 February, 1871, a large fleet of 400 colliers left the Tyne on its journey to Paris, which was under Prussian siege and desperately short of coal. As the fleet arrived at Bridlington the wind dropped and the ships anchored in the bay, awaiting a favourable wind. Early the following morning a north-easterly gale sprang up and, when it swung to the south-east, the vessels were trapped between the shore and Smethwick Sands. They ran for the beach to save breaking up at anchor. Those which did make the beach disintegrated on impact and many that did not foundered in the bay. It was a disaster of mammoth proportions in full sight of the public.

Thirty ships were wrecked in Bridlington Bay and seventy lives were lost — at least, that was the number buried in a mass grave at Bridlington. Further down the Holderness coast, at least a hundred ships were known to have foundered and no one dared to estimate the total loss of life.

This tragedy enraged the nation, particularly when it was made known that, had the vessels been seaworthy, they would probably have survived.

Samuel Plimsoll presented his Bill to the House, using this disaster as his main support; it went through without a division and thus, in 1876, the first Merchant Navy Act became law. It was a comprehensive Act, covering many aspects, but the two most important were:

(1) No vessel may apply for trade or put to sea without a Certificate of Seaworthiness from the Board of Trade.

(2) No vessel may put to sea over or under-loaded and to enforce this 'Load Lines' are required to be painted on all vessels (these are now generally known as 'Plimsoll Lines').

This Act was effective and loss of life at sea was cut down dramatically, though, paradoxically, the number of wrecks on the Holderness coast was not significantly reduced. However, ships usually remained intact on beaching and loss of life became the exception rather than the rule.

The problem was now one of navigation. There was no light between Flamborough Head and Spurn Point, and for a distance between these two lights ships were sailing blind. In north and north-easterly gale conditions they were, unknowingly, swept landwards, the first sign of land being the

Withernsea Pier showing the damage of 28 October, 1880. The Saffron's final resting place.
[Original photograph by George Cammidge]

roar of the breakers. It was then too late. Some of the beached ships were re-floated but many were broken up by the following tides.

And so, what became known as the 'Middle Light Lobby' came into being. Ship owners, sea captains and merchants were all urging the Elder Brethren of Trinity House to station a light between Flamborough and Spurn but, as usual in these cases, publicity was needed to carry the day, and this is where Withernsea pier played its part.

The pier's life was short and dramatic. During a great storm on the night of 28 October, 1880, fifty ships were driven ashore on the Holderness coast. A small fishing smack, the *Jabez*, with a crew of four, hit the end of the pier and sank with all hands. Three of the crew are buried in St. Nicholas' churchyard (near the north-west fence) and the other one at Holmpton, where his body was recovered. The *Saffron*, a coal barque bound for Sunderland from Southampton, had turned to head back for the Humber and safety when its sails were ripped off. It was driven along the coast and struck the pier, punching an eighty-yard gap in the centre before coming to rest on the beach. The crew walked off the ship the following morning! Hornsea pier, 17 miles to the north, was destroyed by the *Earl of Derby* on the same night.

Withernsea pier was quickly repaired with wooden piles and was back in business, but not for long. Less than two years later, during a violent storm

The Leonora *on Withernsea beach.*

on 28 March, 1882, its end section, which included the saloon, was carried away. The vessel responsible was never named. This time, the pier was not repaired but still continued to operate.

During the stormy night of 19 October, 1890, a new fishing smack out of Grimsby, the *Genesta*, was driven ashore at Waxholme. The crew of seven were rescued by the Rocket Brigade but the captain died of exposure in the rigging; at the inquest the coroner remarked that, had there been a light at Withernsea, the tragedy would probably not have occurred. The vessel was beached and, as it was still intact, was auctioned off the following morning to a consortium of local business men. It was not a good bargain! On the following night came another gale and the *Genesta* was driven along the coast at great speed until it met the pier and successfully reduced its length to 90 yards. The pier was now a poor truncated thing, still a pier but only just.

Less than three years later, on the night of 22 March, 1893, the wreckage of a steel ship, whose crew had been rescued earlier, was driven down the coast. It hit the pier like an express train and amidst showers of sparks and tremendous noise brought down span after span until only a twisted mass of metal remained. It was a bright moonlight night and it would seem that the whole population of Withernsea turned out to enjoy the display. The popular press had a field day. There is some debate as to the vessel's name — *Dido* or *Henry Parr*. Whatever its title, it did a thorough demolition job on Withernsea pier: to such effect that the people of Withernsea awoke on the morning of 23 March to find that they no longer had a pier. All that remained were the entrance towers.

A sad end to a brave enterprise! But its history of disasters made excellent copy for the newspapers of the day, which in turn brought to light the desperate need for another lighthouse on the Holderness coast. And on this, the Elder Brethren of Trinity House decided to build a lighthouse at Withernsea.

☆ ☆ ☆ ☆ ☆

The lighthouse took about eighteen months to build and its light first shone across the North Sea at sunset on 1 March, 1894. From the beginning it dominated the town with the sweep of its strangely re-assuring beam and continued to do so, without fail, for the next 82 years, except for the blackout periods during the two world wars.

Built of brick and concrete with octagonal walls, five feet thick, this tall tapering tower was architecturally unusual in Britain and was much admired. It has always been painted white. The foundations are fifteen feet deep with an overall height of a hundred and twenty feet, or a hundred and twenty seven feet above mean high water mark.

It is claimed to be the only lighthouse with a town between it and the sea (the builders obviously having little faith in Withernsea's sea defences!) A spiral staircase of 144 steps on the interior walls leads to the light room and the viewing platform, both a hundred and thirteen feet above mean high water mark. The whole is topped with a wind vane in the shape of a golden arrow, exactly six feet long and weighing two hundredweights. This is connected to a compass in the light room.

The original light was an eight-wick paraffin lamp, housed within an octagonal revolving lens with a bull's eye on each side. The lens, weighing two tons, floated on a trough of three gallons of mercury and was turned by the action of a two-hundredweight weight suspended down the centre of the tower. It took twenty-four seconds for a complete turn of the lens, which was timed each evening by a stop watch. Each flash was thereby synchronised with each bull's eye, giving a sweep of light every three seconds. The range of the light was seventeen miles on a clear night.

The controlling mechanism was always clockwork and required winding daily by hand to bring the weight to the top; this gave turning power for fourteen hours. During the daytime a curtain was drawn to protect the lens from the sun, which would otherwise have concentrated on the bull's eye like a burning glass. The landward side of the light room was shuttered by a steel curtain to prevent the light from shining inland.

Originally there were two keepers, Mr. W. J. Rees and Mr. W. Robins, who lived in the house and cottage attached to the lighthouse. They each had a daughter, ladies who were well known as teachers at the school.

This new middle light was immediately effective, and shipwrecks on the Holderness coast, once commonplace, became a rarity: so much so that the previously overworked Withernsea lifeboat was becoming an anachronism and was eventually withdrawn from service by the R.N.L.I. In 1913, on a bright sunny day in May, the *Docea Chapman*, Withernsea's fifth and last lifeboat, was brought out of its boathouse for the last time and taken by road to Easington, and so an era ended — Withernsea no longer had a lifeboat. To the townspeople its departure was impossible to contemplate and they were angry and dismayed. They had loved their lifeboat and tears were shed as it passed out of the town and out of their lives. Such is progress.

In 1974, as is so often the case, history turned full circle and Withernsea was reopened as a lifeboat station. An inshore rescue boat, very different from the early pulling boats, now operates during the summer season. The crews, as in former times, are all local volunteers, and so, after 61 years, the old tradition prevails.

In 1936 the light was electrified and the paraffin lamp was replaced by a 100-volt, 1500 watt bulb of 800,000 candle power. Had the bulb failed, a second bulb would automatically have moved into place, and, should the main electricity fail, a third bulb, lit by a bank of twenty-six re-chargeable batteries, would immediately come into play. A stand-by generator was provided for emergency use and, as a last resort, the old paraffin lamp was

A famous Withernsea family: (left to right) Kay, Gladys, and Kim Kendall.

retained in reserve. With such precautions the mariners of England were surely secure.

By the 1970s navigational aids both ashore and afloat were casting doubt on the necessity for shore lights, and Trinity House began closing down lighthouses. Withernsea's turn came, and on 1 July, 1976, its light shone for the last time, and another era of Withernsea's story ended.

What was to be the fate of this massive empty edifice — a monument to the past but one which required costly maintenance and now served no useful purpose? Fortunately rescue was on the way.

Most people will recall, or, if too young to remember, will have heard of Kay Kendall, the world-famous actress and film star of the immediate post-World War II period. What many will not know, however, is that she was born in Withernsea and spent most of her childhood there. Her grandfather was Robert Drewery, the patriarch of the last of the Withernsea fishing families and the lifeboat's last coxwain. The Drewerys are direct descendants of Captain James Cook of *Endeavour* fame through the distaff side of the family. Kay, like most of Withernsea's children, had a strong attachment to her birthplace and returned frequently to relax and re-live her idyllic childhood (her words) right up to the time of her tragic and early death in 1959.

She never forgot Withernsea, nor did her mother and her almost equally famous sister, Kim. Her mother, after a varied and interesting life, has returned to live in Withernsea, where she was born, and Kim, and her American husband (Dr. Rolla D. Campbell Junr., M.D.), have taken over the lighthouse. They plan to establish it as a museum, featuring, in particular, the history of Withernsea's lifeboats, coupled with a Kay Kendall memorial. It is to be named the Withernsea Lighthouse Trust, with charitable status and a full board of directors. Dr. and Mrs. Campbell make frequent journeys to Withernsea from their home in Florida and plan to open the lighthouse to the public in the spring of 1989.

It is in keeping with the tradition of the town and of the affection held for it by so many that its most prominent building should be rescued by one of its most famous families.

☆　☆　☆　☆　☆

After the loss of the pier little more is heard of the Withernsea Improvement Company. It had served its purpose and, although it was not exactly a profitable concern, Withernsea was the better for its inception. James Young and his colleagues disappeared from view and no more was heard of them. They were not, however, entirely forgotten; although few people today will have heard of James Young, his name lives on in Young Street.

Although by 1891 the population had risen to 933, there was little further

Kay Kendall with Rex Harrison.

South Promenade, Withernsea.

development for some years and Withernsea appeared destined to remain little more than a village, enlivened in the summer season by day trippers and a few visitors from Hull. The Queen's Hotel was too large and costly for this small resort and was put up for sale.

The main problem was that Withernsea and Owthorne, although they had long since merged into one township, were still operating as two separate villages, each governed by its own parish officers. The parish boundaries were separated by an ancient waterway, leading from the rump end of the mere, later to be the Valley Gardens and the Bowling Green. This waterway was the same 'creke' mentioned earlier in the Elizabethan edict. It is still there, but, like the Fleet in London, is largely built over. It re-appears as the deep drain running to the north of, and adjacent to, the railway track, leading eventually to Winestead Drain. It was originally the main source of water supply to the two villages and, in living memory, a pump stood in the centre of the present crossroads of Queen Street and Seaside Road.

What is now the Alexandra Hotel straddled this waterway, and the first landlord is reputed to have paid rates to both parishes. The Alexandra's present sign requires some explanation: it shows a stream, crossed by a stone bridge and a gate, with a goat standing by. The original building which stood there until 1866, known as the *Got and Gate House*, had nothing to do with either a gate or a goat, but represented a feature of the district.

St. Nicholas' Church and Convalescent Home, c.1900.

The word 'gate' has two meanings:
(1) A way, a road, as in Westgate, derived from 'Dan Gata'.
(2) A right of pasture or stray for cattle. The grazing of this highway was let to cottagers for their cows during the summer and letting was called 'letting the gates'.

'Gote' is the word for a stream or a drain, derived from 'Dan Gjot'. These terms are pure Danish, which would appear to conflict with the fact that Whithornsea was a Saxon holding and requires an explanation. See Appendix B for clarification.

The main road which ran through Withernsea and Owthorne would have crossed this ancient waterway at the boundary. It would almost certainly have been much wider and deeper than it is today. The side verges of the highway would have been used by the villages to graze their cattle, which probably explains the width of Queen Street compared with the main streets of other similar townships of ancient origin, such as Aldbrough and Hornsea. Little is known of the original house or its occupants, except that it was large and that its roof was thatched. When the Hull Brewery Company took it over in 1871 and established it as a hotel, it was probably derelict and required re-building.

In 1898 the two parishes of Withernsea and Owthorne were at last merged into a single urban district, ruled by an elected council. The town re-awakened and a new surge of development followed. By 1901 the population had leapt to 1,426 and was still increasing. A new body of men had taken over the affairs of the town: the first of the many energetic and imaginative Withernsea councils. Each man was a character in his own right and each merits a chapter in this book. Unfortunately, this is denied by lack of space.

Withernsea society has always been unusually egalitarian, and this pattern is illustrated by its early councils. We see rich Hull merchants who built their impressive houses and boathouses at Withernsea deliberating on equal terms with the local window cleaner. The latter happened to be the chairman of the council — an interesting situation, considering that quite a rigid class system prevailed in Britain at that time.

It would seem that, when one stepped off the train at Withernsea, all trappings of power and authority were discarded and one reverted to being a member of Withernsea's extended family. This indefinable feeling of belonging prevails to this day and is surely the reason why so many of its 'children' return to Withernsea in the evening of their lives.

Withernsea's progress was now steady and sure. The Holderness Gas Company Ltd. was established in 1904, and thereafter the town's streets and houses were well lit by gas. By 1921 the population had more than trebled to 4,701, and it remained steady at that figure, rising slowly to 5,098 by 1951 and to 5,974 by 1981. By 1920 new streets and houses were built, the sea wall and promenade was extended to a mile and a quarter, and the

Tom Hart, the butcher, Queen Street (North).

*A late Victorian picture of Queen Street. Note the Alexandra Hotel
(tall building with cornerstones).*

swimming pool had been opened in 1911. At about the same time, a bowling green, tennis courts and a nine-hole golf course were established.

The swimming pool is interesting in its uniqueness. It was built by a wealthy ship owner, Mr. Vickers Walker, who almost immediately leased it to the council at a peppercorn rent, with the proviso that it should always be used exclusively as a swimming pool. It is now owned by the council and is still in use. Initially it was filled with sea water which was changed with each tide by an ingenious system of piping and non-return valves. This was replaced some years ago and fresh water is now used.

The problem of the elegant but empty Queen's Hotel was eventually and finally solved. Sir James and Mr. Francis Reckitt, those great late-Victorian/Edwardian philanthropists, were anxious to provide a convalescent home for the poor people of Hull, where they could recuperate after serious illness. Consumption was rampant in Hull and the medical profession of the day concluded that the only cure was fresh air and rest. The 'pure life-giving air' of Withernsea was recommended, so the Reckitts bought the Queen's Hotel and in 1902 presented it to Hull Royal Infirmary. In 1903 Withernsea Convalescent Home was duly opened by Lord Herries and successfully continued for many decades. It is still in use as the Withernsea Hospital.

Sir James then experimented with the open air treatment of consumption by erecting two large tents in the hospital grounds, followed by the building of a sanatorium at a cost of £3,000 for the treatment of patients. It was one of the first buildings of its type in England and is now converted into a health centre, incorporating G.P. and community health facilities. So the good work of these two great men lives on at Withernsea, even though the scourge of tuberculosis has been defeated. Cuthbert Brodrick's work was not in vain after all. Incidentally, the first matron of the Convalescent Home was named Cavell. She was the sister of the famous Nurse Edith Cavell who was executed as an alleged spy by the Germans in 1915 during the First World War. A fine statue of her stands close to Trafalgar Square in London.

In 1916 a water tower was erected at Rimswell, and Withernsea was supplied with water from Hull by a nine-inch pipe. This water was too hard for some residents, who objected strongly to losing the soft spring water from their pumps. Nevertheless, the tower was essential if this expanding town was not to develop a water-supply problem.

By the 1920s Withernsea was established as a quiet, family seaside resort, making no pretensions to be a Filey or a Bridlington; its brochures concentrated on extolling the virtues of the fresh, health-giving ozone and expansive sandy beaches. That is not to say that no entertainment was provided, although this was unsophisticated by the standards of the more elegant resorts. Catlin's Pierrots had been established since 1905, performing daily throughout the season on a makeshift stage on the beach, and in the evenings vaudeville shows were to be enjoyed in the Floral Hall.

Withernsea before the First World War.

Catlins Royal Pierrots, c.1907.

South Cliff, 1920's.

Not a brilliant picture — but it proves how popular Withernsea became!

Donkey rides, round-abouts and swings on the beach, swimming galas, regattas and exhibitions were all available for the crowds who surged into the town in the summer season. In the three months of June, July and August, 1925, almost 200,000 passengers travelled by rail from Hull to Withernsea (more than two-thirds of the population of Hull at that time). The people of Hull had indeed made Withernsea their own. Few who spent their childhood in Hull during the 1920s and 1930s will not look back with nostalgia on their days by the sea at Withernsea.

At about this time the annual Withernsea Carnival was introduced (it still continues today). Almost everybody, especially the children, dressed up in fancy costumes and entered the simple competitions with gusto, in a happy, good-natured week of revelry. Many of the pierrots and vaudeville actors went on to be well-known figures in the entertainment world. One such, Donald Pears of *By a Babbling Brook* fame, lodged with Mrs. G. Boyden in Cammidge Street during the season.

From early days, Withernsea had a town band. It was well-trained and appeared in its smart blue uniforms on any and every occasion, particularly on the band stand on Sunday afternoons and Bank Holidays. One of Withernsea's famous sons, Kenny Baker, is reputed to have learnt to play the trumpet with the band. He was to become Britain's leading trumpeter. It is interesting to note that, when Kay Kendall played that marvellous piece on the trumpet in the film *Genevieve*, the actual player was Kenny Baker; Kay, of course, was miming. One wonders what reminiscences of Withernsea went on off camera.

☆　☆　☆　☆　☆

In 1934 Winifred Holtby stayed at Withernsea from mid-March to early June, where she gathered material for her best-selling novel, *South Riding*. She lived at *Delma*, now 27, Waxholme Road, the present home of Mr. and Mrs. Edward Marshall. The town of 'Kiplington' in her novel is easily identified as Withernsea, (although aspects of Bridlington and Hornsea are captured), and one can recognize the locality and even some of the characters. Anyone living at Withernsea during the 1930s would probably agree that she painted a somewhat gloomy picture of Holderness; but, then, Winifred was writing a novel, not history; she did, however, enjoy her stay at Withernsea and praised its wild beauty. She died in 1935, one month after completing *South Riding*. It was published in 1936 and was an immediate best-seller, winning the James Tait Black Memorial Prize in 1937. Most critics consider it to be her finest work.

A commemorative plaque, recently organized by the Winifred Holtby Committee and presented by Humberside County Council, is now displayed at 27, Waxholme Road.

☆　☆　☆　☆　☆

No. 27 Waxholme Road,
rented by Winifred Holtby, 1934.

Cecil Rhodes, J.P.

Unlike many seaside resorts, Withernsea did not die in the winter months. It remained a lively place and the residents continued to enjoy themselves. The rinks, cinemas, various societies, whist drives, church and chapel occasions, dances and other activities continued. In fact, many residents preferred the autumn and winter, for the town was their own again.

Although roller skating had lost its popularity by the early 1930s, the large wooden rink adjoining the station remained the focal point of entertainment, and the Saturday night dances were a 'must' for the young — and the not so young. It was, therefore, a bitter blow when the place was burnt to the ground in the late 1930s. With typical enterprise, it was quickly replaced by the magnificent Grand Pavilion which, with its superb maple dance floor, was claimed to be the largest and finest dance hall on the east coast. It attracted people from far and wide and greatly enhanced Withernsea's reputation. It was built almost entirely through the initiative and determination of Cecil Rhodes, a fruit merchant of Hull who lived at Withernsea. He was a Withernsea councillor of great sagacity and surmounted the problems of, and opposition to, his enterprise with a stubborn disregard for all difficulties and discouragement. It was fitting that a plaque in his honour was built into the front entrance of the Grand Pavilion.

At the outbreak of war in 1939 all seaside resorts were closed for the duration, the beaches being wired off and entrance forbidden to the public. Like the rest of Britain, Withernsea emerged from the war in a rundown and shabby condition, badly in need of a face lift. In spite of heroic efforts, rehabilitation was slow and painful; money was in short supply and material was almost unobtainable. Nevertheless, by the 1950s much had been accomplished and Withernsea was again a seaside resort. But not in the style and fashion as before.

The pierrots and vaudeville acts never returned and visitors seemed disinclined to spend the whole day on the beach; no longer was the sea front black with people. The roundabouts and the other numerous beach entertainments had gone, and with them the old atmosphere of innocence. The people of Hull still crowded into the resort, but their tastes had changed — the amusement arcades and bingo halls now claimed their attention.

Just as the town was beginning to look like its old self again, it received a blow which staggered the residents. The unbelievable happened — Withernsea lost its railway. In 1964, the Beeching axe fell and the Hull/Withernsea line was discontinued. It was unthinkable, and it was finally accepted only when the track itself was removed. All that remains to remind us that Withernsea once had a railway is a derelict station and a rough cinder track leading to Patrington, and, of course, Railway Crescent.

An open air market which attracts visitors from far afield now operates on the station platform. Whether it is entirely popular with the residents is debatable. Many faint hearts forecast that the loss of the railway foreshadowed the demise of Withernsea; they knew little of the town or of its people. It shook itself, recovered from the shock, and, remarkably, went on with life very much as before. With hindsight, one can see that the shock was largely psychological. Public road transport and the increasing ownership of the motor car quickly replaced the train, and the town was not cut off as feared. Those who remember the railway, however, will still recall

The Grand Pavilion.

46

the delights and convenience of the short journey through Holderness to Hull: no traffic problems, and pleasant company on the way.

In 1974 the Government of the day re-arranged the county boundaries of England and the people of Holderness were told that they were no longer Yorkshiremen; they were to become Humbersiders! More seriously, Withernsea lost its council, and local government became centralized under the Holderness District Council. Withernsea's interests were represented by only four members, out of a total council of thirty-one.

The personal touch, which had bonded the town together for some seventy-six years, had gone, and Withernsea was the poorer for it. Its impressive and historic council chamber was left empty and forlorn, slowly crumbling into dereliction.

Over the following ten years it became increasingly clear that Withernsea needed its own direct representatives, and in 1984 authority was obtained and Withernsea's new parish council, with its own chairman, was duly elected. In 1986 the council was 'promoted' to town council and the chairman became the town mayor. With the re-instatement of its own council in 1984 the effect on the town was almost instant. Long outstanding points of interest and complaint, trivial to outsiders, were put to rights and the townspeople once more had ready access to their councillors. One example can be quoted: the derelict land, once the Memorial Gardens adjacent to the promenade, had long been an eyesore and the subject of

Floral Hall and Memorial.

many complaints, but for various reasons no action seemed possible. It is now embanked and turned into a pleasant area of rest and recreation; all done under the Youth Training Scheme.

The Municipal Buildings, with the council chamber, have been re-furbished and the council can now deliberate in its old dignified home — the town is back to normal.

We are now up-to-date and our brief story is complete.

☆　☆　☆　☆　☆

Withernsea has still retained its 'long straggling' character and still has that unplanned look. No one, no matter how partisan, would call it a beautiful town; and yet it has a certain wild charm and an atmosphere all of its own, and over the decades has captured many hearts. Someone once described it as 'a funny, ugly, lovely little town', so perhaps we should settle for that.

What of its future? Changes are inevitable if places are to remain alive, and, even as one writes, these changes are taking place. A plan to re-develop the town centre has begun and already the Grand Pavilion is gutted, to be transformed into the new leisure centre; the plaque in honour of Cecil Rhodes, previously mentioned, is to be incorporated into the new building. Sensibly, the old derelict station will be preserved. It will be re-furbished in its present form and used as auxiliary accommodation, to include storerooms, toilets and other facilities for the use of the market tradespeople. The old station platform and track is to be converted into an established open market with adequate car parking facilities; and fronting all this, on the Queen Street side, will be a supermarket.

And so the town centre will acquire a new look and the place will never be quite the same again. If only Anthony Bannister could be there to see it! Whatever the future holds and whatever changes take place, that spirit of friendly independence and the extended family tradition, which has sustained Withernsea (and Owthorne) from its earliest days, must NEVER change — nor will it.

Nurse Cavell, Matron of Withernsea Convalescent Home, the sister of Edith Cavell.

The Grand Pavilion under demolition, 1988.

The old Memorial Gardens, after transformation, 1987.

49

Bibliography

Works consulted during the preparation of this book include:

Simon H. Adamson, *Seaside Piers* (1977).
K. J. Allison (ed.), *A History of the County of York — East Riding*, Vol. V Holderness: Southern Part (OUP 1984).
Paul Baker, *Wooden Boats and Men of Steel: The Withernsea Lifeboats 1862-1913* (Withernsea 1984).
Vera Brittain, *Testament of Friendship* (1940).
Robert Carson, *The First Hundred Years* (Middlesbrough 1978).
'A Fellow of the Royal Historical Society', *Holderness and Holdernessians* (1878: Malet Lambert Local History Reprints, Hull, Extra Volumes No. 44).
Arthur Godfrey and Peter J. Lassey, *Shipwrecks of the Yorkshire Coast* (Clapham 1974).
A Popular Guide to the Hull and Holderness Railway with an account of Withernsea (1859: Malet Lambert Local History Reprints, Hull, Extra Volumes No. 37).
George Poulson, *History of Holderness* (Hull, London 1840-1)
Thomas Sheppard, *The Lost Towns of the Yorkshire Coast* (Hull 1912)
Frank Stenton, *Anglo-Saxon England* (Oxford 1943).
Harry Verity, *Founded on the Rock: Withernsea Methodist Church 1879-1979* (Withernsea 1979).
Thomas Walton, *A Day on the Holderness Railway* (1856: Malet Lambert Local History Reprints, Hull, Extra Volumes No. 36).
G. C. Waters (ed.), *Withernsea and its Schools* (Withernsea 1978).

APPENDIX A

Murder at Owthorne

In the year 1690 or thereabouts a young woman was washed up on the beach at Owthorne from the wreck of a ship. She was clutching a young baby and both were taken to the vicarage where the mother died. The baby, however, survived, seemingly little the worse for his ordeal.

No one claimed the child and it was finally decided that he should stay on at the vicarage, not as the vicar's adopted son but as a potential man of all work around the house and grounds; his position was a lowly one and it is not entirely surprising that he grew up to be a morose and sullen youth who was unpopular in the village.

The vicar's household consisted of himself, the Rev. Henock Sinclair, his two nieces, Mary and Catherine Sinclair, and the now grown-up foundling, Adam Alvin. In spite of his surly character, Adam managed to gain the affections of Mary, the elder of the two nieces, much to the annoyance of the vicar who angrily forbade the liaison.

The solution to Adam's problems were simple: he must get rid of the vicar and he proceeded to do this, presumably with the full knowledge and even support of the two nieces.

In early June, 1708, Alvin murdered Henock Sinclair and buried his body in the vicarage garden. He then saddled and bridled the vicar's horse as though for a journey and left it some miles from the village. A report was then circulated that the vicar had set out on a journey the previous day and had disappeared, probably over the cliffs, as his hat and wig were found on the beach. The villagers were suspicious and ugly rumours were circulated associating Adam's name with the vicar's disappearance. Nothing, however, could be proved against him, particularly as the sisters fully supported his story.

Within two months, on 29 August, 1708, Adam and Mary were secretly married at Halsham (six miles from Owthorne) on a special licence. The people of Owthorne were outraged when they learnt of this, and, shortly after, the three conspirators left the district, Alvin and his wife going to reside in London.

Four years later, Catherine Sinclair had a serious illness and, to ease her conscience, she either made a full confession of her part in the crime or indicated where the body could be found. Alvin and his wife were then arrested in London and brought to York for trial. Alvin was convicted, his wife being acquitted.

During the preaching of the condemned sermon, Alvin loudly proclaimed his innocence, which so affected the preacher, the Rev. Mr. Mace, that he had a seizure and fell down dead. 'See', said Alvin, 'the hand of God visibly displayed.' However, when faced with death on the following morning, he fully confessed to the crime and was duly hanged.

Did Adam Alvin plan the murder or did he kill the vicar by accident during one of his many outbursts of uncontrollable temper? Many believed the latter until an early entry in the Owthorne Overseer's Book of 4 May, 1708, was unearthed. This showed the vicar to be in possession of a property of the annual value of £12. In the year after the murder, Mr. Sinclair's name drops out and the name of Adam Alvin appears. It would seem that Alvin, through the rightful claim of his wife, came into some property on the death of the vicar.

So, perhaps Adam's plans were more devious than at first appeared. Whatever the case, he eventually paid for his crime in full measure.

The former bandstand.

APPENDIX B

Although Edward the Confessor was a Saxon King and Whithornsea was a Saxon holding, it was also a Danish settlement under the Danelaw.

This paradox dates back to the time of Alfred, the King of Wessex, and his absolute defeat of Guthrum's Danish army at Ethandun — now Edington — in the year 878. Instead of the customary massacre and banishment which followed most victories in those barbarous days, Alfred uplifted the Danes, converted them to Christianity, gave them land and permitted them to live in peace within their own laws — the Danelaw.

And so, for some eighty years, under the rule of five great Saxon kings, these Danish settlements became deeply rooted in the soil and, together with their Saxon cousins, eventually formed the united English nation of the tenth and eleventh centuries: King Alfred's grandson, Athelstan, became the first king of all England in 937.

As a typical Danish settlement the Whithornsea of those far-off days would have consisted of bands of free men owing allegiance to a leader who allotted rented land to them and demanded their attendance at his court; beyond that they would be free and they could have left their leader if they had wished.

The land was divided into parcels of variable sizes, known as sokes, and the tenants were known as sokemen: a proud title indicating freedom. The Saxon serfs and villeins, who were tied completely and for life to their lords, were unknown under the Danelaw.

Unlike the Saxon laws, Danelaw was administered through the family unit, whose adult members were required to attend the courts of law when one of their members was to be arraigned as a law breaker. Not only were they required to speak up on the miscreant's behalf but they were obliged to stand surety for his future good conduct; in fact, the whole family was on trial. Some historians tell us that this was an early example of the jury system.

All other community activity was also centred on the family, so much so that in many cases small settlements consisted of one extended family unit, the family elders being men of great influence. This free, independent, extended family characteristic continued over the centuries despite the draconian rule of the early Normans.

So we see the Whithornsea of early times as a Saxon holding of Danish origins, ruled entirely by the Danelaw, but firmly under the fief of the Saxon king.

APPENDIX C

Street Names of Withernsea

Street names can be indicative of a town's past; they can also be confusing and misleading if one interprets their origins too literally. The reasons for the names are rarely recorded and often the more 'obvious' reason is the wrong one, and conflicting myths often develop. Nevertheless, street names are of importance and of historical interest and this appendix is produced in order to discuss some of Withernsea's more interesting street names and their implications on its history.

Queen Street

Obviously named after Queen Victoria as the town developed in the second half of the 19th century. The street is, however, an ancient roadway and the town section was merely re-named. Its original title was *Waxholme Road*, being the main highway, passing through Withernsea and Owthorne to Waxholme.

It was cut by the encroaching sea and now comes to an abrupt end at the *North Promenade*. It re-emerges as the original *Waxholme Road* to the north-west of the town and continues on its ancient way.

Arthur Street

An early 19th-century map reveals *Arthur Street* as a short road connecting what is now *Hubert Street* and *Alma Street* at their western ends. It was part of a small farming community consisting of two farms, a manor house, farm cottages and a blacksmith's shop, situated to the west of the old village of Owthorne. These were the only buildings and the enclave was surrounded by fields. It was possibly named after Prince Arthur, the Duke of Connaught, or it could even have been named to honour a local farmer; but we will probably never know.

The present *Arthur Street* was necessary to accommodate the houses newly built at the turn of the 20th century. It stretched from Hull Road to the northern fields, incorporating the old Arthur Street *en route*. It also, somewhat unimaginatively, stole its name.

North Road

Built in 1916 to connect with *Waxholme Road* and *Arthur Street*. Previously the old *Waxholme Road* ended at the cliff face and there was no connecting road between Withernsea and Waxholme. The name *North Road* merely indicates a road to the North.

Alma Street

Previously *Williamson* or *William Street*. In early days a butcher's shop-cum-ale-house stood at its north-eastern corner with a slaughter house to the rear. In 1864, Mr. Henry Greensides, a former farm bailiff to Count Zelinski of Hungary, came to Withernsea and took over these premises, from which, at first, he traded in farm machinery. He also continued with the alehouse which soon developed into a well-known public house named the Alma, after the 1854 battle during the recent Crimean War. *Williamson Street* then became *Alma Street*. The Alma Hotel is still with us, its proprietor being Mr. Bryan Greensides, the great-grandson of its original landlord.

It is not known who the Williamson was who gave the street its first name. He was probably a land owner, maybe a local farmer.

Hubert Street

Originally *Kingston Street* — changed later to *Princess* Street, almost certainly named after one of the royal princesses. 'Kingston Lodge' was the name of Anthony Bannister's residence in Hessle! Major Robson, of the Moors and Robson brewery family, took up residence in Withernsea and had a large house built at the north-eastern corner of Princess Street; he named it Hubert House after his youngest son, Hubert. The town's development in the southern sector came later, when Princes Avenue appears with its more gracious dwellings. The two street names were too similar, confusion followed and so Princess Street was re-named *Hubert Street*. Hubert House later became Owthorne Manor, which causes many to mistakenly believe it to be the ancient manor of old Owthorne.

North Gate

The shortest street in Withernsea, being all that is left of the *Barb Lane* of old Owthorne; the remainder disappeared into the sea long ago. Originally it led due east from *Waxholme Road* as part of the street system of Owthorne. It would have been lined with dwellings, built mainly of beach cobbles and usually of a single-storey; two of these are still in existence, both in good condition and occupied.

Barb Lane was changed to *North Gate* in the 19th century. It is an apt name for this short gateway to the North Sea. The origin of the name *Barb Lane* is lost in the mists of time, but *possibly* it indicated a lane lined with thorn bushes.

Cammidge Street

George Cammidge, the builder, was responsible for much of the northern development of the new town, and, as was fashionable in those days, this new street took his name.

George Street

A short street connecting *Alma Street* and *Cammidge Street*. It was named after the same George Cammidge — not a King!

High Brighton Street

The early founders of the new Withernsea hoped to emulate the small village of Brightlingsea in Sussex, which emerged as the famous royal watering place of Brighton, and High Brighton is probably meant to indicate the Brighton of the North.

Bannister Street

Named after Anthony Bannister, who brought the railway to Withernsea. Shown on the original plan as *Esplanade*.

Young Street

Named after James Young, who was the chairman of the Withernsea Improvement Company during its most successful period.

☆   ☆   ☆   ☆   ☆

In the early 1900s, avenues were becoming fashionable addresses and we can see how this influenced the later development in the southern sector of Withernsea.

Victoria Avenue

An obvious name relating to Queen Victoria.

Park Avenue

A splendid name for a rather gracious avenue, but with no park at its end. Perhaps it was intended to build a park later; there was certainly enough land. Or maybe the name just sounded attractive.

Cheverton Avenue

Named after Mr. Martin Cheverton-Brown, one of the many eminent and wealthy men who took up residence in Withernsea during the late 19th century. He was a prominent financier who took an active part in the town's affairs, being four times the chairman of Withernsea's council (1901-1906-1911-1912).

The grounds of his large house stretched down to the cliff face where he had built a private boathouse and slipway. He later sold his property to the council, when it became the town's Municipal Buildings, containing the

56

council chamber; it remains so to this day. The grounds were later developed into the present Italian Gardens, and, much later, the present Teddy's Club occupied the site of the boathouse.

Memorial Avenue

The war memorial to the fallen in World War I was erected near to the short roadway opposite the station. This rough, sandy track was built into a metalled road and named accordingly. The war memorial was later re-sited behind the Municipal Buildings.

Lascelles Avenue

This is the service road to a double row of well-appointed houses, built in the 1920s to the south of Hull Road. It was so named to celebrate the marriage of the Princess Royal to Lord Harewood in 1922, the Harewood family name being Lascelles.

Lee Avenue

To date no trace of its origin can be found.

Chestnut Avenue

A well-sounding name which was popular in many suburban developments. In this case, it could possibly refer to nearby horse chestnut trees in the area now occupied by a garage.

Louville Avenue

Most probably this was an invented title, but the derivation of *Louville* is obscure.

Piggy Lane

A rough road leading westwards from Queen Street, near to the station. It now leads to a footpath into the centre of Lascelles Avenue. Pigs were kept at its western end within living memory, the last pig-keeper being Dick Woodhouse in the 1920s.

Turner Avenue

Part of a 1970s housing development in the area of Holmpton Road. It was named in honour of Councillor Harold Turner, who has served Withernsea as a councillor for many years, and is still doing so. It is a rare honour to name a street after a person who is not only still living but who also remains in active service to the community.

APPENDIX D

A Withernsea Chronology

1047-1066 First mention of Whithornsea in reign of Edward the Confessor.

1444   Great floods.

1488   St. Nicholas' Church dedicated.

1609   Great storm.

1816   Disappearance of St. Peter's Church, Owthorne.

1854   Opening of railway.

1859   St. Nicholas' Church re-dedicated.

1862   First lifeboat at Withernsea.

1873   First newspaper — *Withernsea Chronicle*.

1877   Pier and promenade completed.

1878   Board School opened.

1880   Pier damaged.

1893   Pier finally destroyed.

1894   Lighthouse in use.

1964   Railway closed.

1976   Lighthouse closed.

1986   Town Council established.